Read Your Bible

The Lens With Which We View And Understand Everything

How to read and understand the Word of God

By

Tiffany McInnes

www.TheLiteralWord.com

Read Your Bible
The Lens With Which We View And Understand Everything
How to read and understand the Word of God

Copyright ©2024 Tiffany McInnes
All rights reserved

Scripture quotations from The Holy Bible, English Standard Version.

<u>Dedication</u>

I'd like to give all glory and recognition to the One
True God, The Father, The Son and The Holy Spirit,
to whom I owe everything.

Foreword

I am deeply proud of my wife Tiffany for tackling this much needed book which has been on her heart for so long. As Christians it is vitally important that we are connected to God. After all, Christianity is a relationship. Good relationships require among other things good communication and knowledge of one another. God gave us the Bible so that we could know Him, and He could tell us His will. He gave us prayer so we could speak to Him. And He gave us the Holy Spirit and meditation/quiet time so that we could hear from Him. But the greatest foundational discipline is to read and understand the scriptures. This is how we not only know God, but how we know the will of God and how we have discernment to know when He is speaking to us. If we lack this foundation we may struggle to know if we're hearing from the Holy Spirit or from an unholy spirit.

This book will help you learn to love reading and studying the bible. I hope that once you are putting God and His Word in their rightful place in your life, above everything else, your personal and miraculous relationship with our amazing Lord blooms and you search the scriptures with your whole heart to know the One True God!

If we truly know how big and how great God is, when it comes to reading, quiet time and prayer, we'll stop saying "I need to find more time for God" and start saying, "I need to find more time for everything else!"

God bless you.

Table of Contents

Introduction

The purpose of this book is to help you not only
understand your Bible but to fall in love with reading
your Bible, worshiping God through reading it, and
receiving the full Glory of God in His living, inerrant,
infallible, written Word. The Bible is real, it is Truth,
and it is ALL about Jesus.

Remember, it's not about improving self, it's about
dying to self and living for Christ. How do we live for
Christ? We submit to His Word daily. How do you
submit to His Word daily? READ YOUR BIBLE!
Read it to see and understand His Glory. The Glory
that will transform you to be more like Him and a lot
less like you. I don't want to apply things to my life, I
want a new life, a new life in Christ. Stop reading your
Bible for self application and start reading it to fear
God and to see His Glory. Other books, blogs,
sermons, reels and podcasts, as clever and inspiring as
they may seem, are not the infallible, inerrant Word of

God. They cannot change you, they will only help your *self*. Don't forget to read the WHOLE Bible. The full gospel of Truth. He's the same yesterday, today, and always. The God of the Old Testament is the same God of the New Testament. Take Him at His Word. He is 100% accurate 100% of the time. The Bible may be difficult to understand sometimes, but difficult does not mean contradictory. God's Word will NOT contradict itself.

Please start by asking yourself these questions:

1. Do you believe all scripture to be the written <u>inerrant</u> Word of God?

*Inerrant = it is the final authority and is without error or fault in all its teachings. See 2 Timothy 3:16

2. Do you believe all scripture to be the <u>infallible</u> Word of God?

*Infallible = incapable of error; incapable of being wrong or making a mistake

3. Do you believe God is 100% accurate 100% of
   the time?

4. Do you believe the Bible is Truth?
If you answered NO to ANY of these questions you
are calling God a liar. Be careful of the ground you
walk on.

If you answered YES to ALL of these questions you
have to take Him at His Word; all scripture,
LITERALLY!

What do I mean when I say literally? We will talk more
extensively about this in chapter 3, but a literal
interpretation means you interpret scripture with a
historical, grammatical, contextual interpretation.
Letting scripture interpret scripture. This does not
negate poetry, songs, similes, figures of speech or
symbols.

Before moving forward, if you do not have the Holy
Spirit you can not have the wisdom and the
discernment to fully understand scripture. If you have
never accepted Jesus Christ as your personal Lord and
Savior, repented of your sins, turned from your wicked
ways, and received His forgiveness by His death and

resurrection on the cross, PLEASE turn first to the back of this book and learn how you can have hope in Jesus Christ and receive the Holy Spirit.

WARNING: Do not listen to public speakers, teachers, and even pastors who do not have the Holy Spirit. There are many wolves in sheep's clothing but also wolves in shepherds' clothing too.
As you read your Bible and study His Word, ask the Holy Spirit for wisdom and understanding. He will equip you with the discernment to know false teachings. Remember, the Bible is the lens with which you view and understand everything!

"The fear of the Lord is the beginning of knowledge; fools despise wisdom and instruction." Proverbs 1:7

Fear God. Be encouraged. And READ YOUR BIBLE!

Chapter 1
Navigating the Bible

"God made the Bible so simple that even an intellectual can understand it." ~Mark Fischer

The Bible is much more than a book, it is a library of books, and books written in different literary forms. Some portions of the Bible give a historical account, others poetic, and some are prophetic. (Ref: David Guzik, Enduring Word Commentary)

All scripture is breathed out by God as II Timothy 3:16-17 tells us, *"All scripture is breathed out by God and is profitable for teaching, for reproof, for correction, and for training in righteousness, that the man of God may be competent, equipped for every good work."*

Let's start with the basics and turn to your Bible's Table of Contents so we can get the "lay of the land". This is located at the beginning of your Bible.

The Bible has 66 books in total.

You will see a heading labeled Old Testament. The Old Testament, also referred to as the Old Covenant, has 39 books.

The first five books are what we call the Books of Moses or the Torah. These are; Genesis, Exodus, Leviticus, Numbers and Deuteronomy.

The next twelve books, Joshua to Esther, are historical accounts of the Jewish wars, judges and kings of Israel.

Job, Psalms, Proverbs, Ecclesiastes, and Song of Solomon are poetic books.

Then we get into the five major prophets, which are not major because of importance but because of the length of each book. These are Isaiah, Jeremiah, Lamentations, Ezekiel and Daniel.

Finishing out the Old Testament are the twelve minor prophets, Hosea to Malachi. They are not minor in importance but in the length of each book.

There are 400 years between the end of the Old Testament and the beginning of the New Testament.

The New Testament, also referred to as the New Covenant, has twenty seven books in total.

The first four books, Matthew, Mark, Luke, and John are called the Gospels. The Gospels are historical books and they record the life and teachings of Jesus.

The book of Acts, is the acts of the apostles and provides an account of the beginning of the Church.

Romans to Philemon are the thirteen letters written by the apostle Paul. They are sometimes referred to as the Epistles, the Epistles of Paul or the Pauline Epistles.

Hebrews to the last book of the Bible, Revelation, are nine letters written by other apostles.

Fun fact: 28% of the Bible is prophecy.

As you read the Old Testament and into the New Testament keep in mind that the God of the Old Testament is the same God of the New Testament. He is unchanging, unwavering, and faithful to ALL His promises. Also, look for Jesus in every book. Don't forget, it's all about Jesus! Amen!

Chapter 2
The Glory of God's Word

Plan to meet God, and to see and know His glory.

The number 1 thing to remember when reading
scripture is it's all about His glory and for His glory.
Before you begin reading the Bible, each time;
-Pray
-Invite Him to meet with you
-Ask for wisdom and understanding

Beginning with prayer is so important. Before opening
the Word of God, humbly present yourself to God.
Being in a posture of humility sets our hearts right to
meet God in His rightful position above us and
everything else.

Invite Him into your time in the Word. Even though it
is His Word, we forget to invite Him to be present.
His Word is living and Jesus is the active ingredient to

this beautiful array of God's Glory and presence.
Invite Him into your time together. Again, this sets
your heart and mind in a humbleness needed to be in
the presence of our Holy God.

Specifically ask for wisdom and understanding to
discern the Truths of God's Word. Proverbs 3:13 says;
*"Blessed is the one who finds wisdom, and the one who
gets understanding".*

As we live in unparalleled times and the world
continues to call good evil, and evil good, we need His
wisdom and understanding of Truth so we do not get
deceived by the half-truth or the almost-truth that the
world and even our churches are teaching and
preaching.

Proverbs 1:28-31; *"Then they will call upon me, but I
will not answer; they will seek me diligently but will not
find me. Because they hated knowledge and did not
choose the fear of the Lord, would have none of my
counsel and despised all my reproof, therefore they shall
eat the fruit of their own way, and have their fill of their
own devices."*

This generation has replaced the fear of God with the grace of God, and we need to understand that one can not negate the other.

The Bible is not a self help book. As much as pastors these days preach with the main focus of their sermons being life application, this should not be why we read and study His Word. The Bible is written to know God's Glory, and then by His Glory we are changed and transformed.

When we go to the Bible looking to help ourselves the focus becomes SELF. We place ourselves in God's position. The god of self, which we see so much of in today's churches and society. Our bookshelves are covered in self-help, self-care, self-reliance books. This trusting in "self-help" is a false teaching and is a direct deception of Satan.

Galatians 1:6-10; *"I am astonished that you are so quickly deserting him who called you in the grace of Christ and are turning to a different gospel- not that there is another one, but there are some who trouble you and want to distort the gospel of Christ. But even if we or an angel from heaven should preach to you a gospel contrary to the one we preached to you, let him be accursed. As we have said before, so now I say again: If anyone is preaching to you a gospel contrary to the one you received, let him be accursed. For am I now seeking the approval of man, or of God? Or am I trying to please man? If I were trying to please man, I would not be a servant of Christ."*

When we go to the Bible looking to see God's Glory we learn to fear Him and place God in His rightful position in our lives. We need to always put God in His rightful position in our lives and in scripture, above everything including self. John 3:30 says; *He must increase, but I must decrease.*

As you read scripture, whether it be a verse, a chapter, or a book, start with:

How does this passage,
1. Reveal God's Glory?
2. Exalt God's Glory?
3. Highlight Jesus?

The application of scripture does not need to be sought after, rather the revealing, exalting and glorifying of the name above every other name, Jesus, should be sought after, and by the overwhelming infiltration of the holiness of God's immeasurable glory bestowed on us by the sacrifice of His perfect son, the Lamb of God, will inevitably and supernaturally be applied to our lives through the death of self and the life of Christ.

Jude 24;

"Now to him who is able to keep you from stumbling and to present you blameless before the presence of his glory with great joy, to the only God, our Savior, through Jesus Christ our Lord, be glory, majesty, dominion, and authority, before all time and now and forever. Amen."

Chapter 3
The Literal Word

God says what He means and means what He says.
-Mark Fischer

We discussed this briefly in the introduction of this book but now we get to dive fully into it - The literal interpretation of scripture. A large number of today's churches use an allegorical approach to interpret scripture and this is why I feel that it is of the utmost importance to address how we need to interpret the Bible literally. In this chapter we will discuss why we should not interpret scripture allegorically and what does literal vs allegorical really mean.

Simply put, the literal approach relies on the text for meaning. The allegorical approach relies on the interpreter for meaning. This is a very important distinction.

If you had a table full of people, and they all took the Bible literally, they would all come up with the same interpretation. Start to finish. But if that same table of people all took the Bible, or even part of the Bible, allegorically they would, undoubtedly, ALL come up with their own interpretation. You'd have a table full of different interpretations, each person with their own.

Do you think God intended for His Word to be left to many "truths" or do you think there is one truth, thee Truth? God is not a God of confusion. He wants us to know the Truth. He is not inconsistent. Satan is the father of lies and confusion. And this attack has been on the church since day one. Again, this is why it is so important that you know your Bible and you are in God's Word daily. Taking Him at His Word.

My father, Mark Fischer, wrote a book on Revelation in 2012, called Advance Notice: Jesus Wins! In his book he writes about the literal interpretation, and because I couldn't write it better I am going to refer to his writings for the remainder of this chapter.
[Ref: Advance Notice: Jesus Wins! A Journey Through Revelation Into the Future by Mark Fischer, (2012) pgs 28-31.]

Dr David L Cooper (1886-1965), founder of the Biblical Research Society taught as his golden rule of interpretation: *"when the plain sense of the scripture makes common sense, seek no other sense; therefore, take every word at its primary, ordinary, usual, literal meaning unless the facts of the immediate text, studied in the light of related passages and axiomatic (self-evident) and fundamental truths, clearly indicates otherwise."*

We should seek to know first what a passage actually means; who, whom, what, where, when, why before we make an application. [That is Who wrote it, to Whom were they writing it, What was happening that was relevant at the time, Where were they, When did they write it and Why were they writing it.] If we don't use this contextual ground work when reading scripture, the passage would be fundamentally useless because the author's intent would be lost. We would then come up with many and bizarre applications God might never have intended.

In his book, Things to Come (Grand Rapids Dunham, 1964 p9), J.D. Pentecost says, *"The literal method of interpretation is that method that gives to each word the exact basic meaning it would have in normal, ordinary, customary usage...it is called the grammatical historical method to emphasize that the meaning is to be determined by both grammatical and historical consideration."*

At the heart of it all, God wants us first to understand <u>and then</u> apply what He's revealed.

By literal, I don't mean a rigid, mechanical interpretation that rules out figures of speech and symbols. Within the literal context various figures of speech may be used to make a point. This is common to all languages. When dealing with these cases there is usually a contextual clue, such as the word "like". For example, in Matthew 13:24, Jesus said, "the kingdom of heaven is <u>like</u> a man who sowed good seed in the field." The word "like" in this context tips us off to the fact that this is a simile - a figure of speech.

Please remember, that for a symbol to be a symbol it must symbolize something of literal truth.

There is no need to fabricate a mystical meaning. I advocate using a contextual approach to evaluate symbolism.

1) The immediate context
2) The whole book context
3) The whole Bible context

Ask yourself, is my interpretation of the symbol consistent with the passage in which it's found? Also, was it used elsewhere in scripture? Where? How? Nearly every symbol is seen and explained somewhere in the text. We must always exercise due diligence in these matters. Look up the original and historical meanings of the word. Inspiration and interpretation are both vitally important.

Let's look at an example. In Matthew 5:30 Jesus says, *"And if your right hand causes you to sin, cut it off and cast it from you"*. If you stopped reading there, you may think literally Jesus is telling people to cut off their hands if they do wicked. But two things, first we know from a whole book and a whole bible context that cutting off your hand is not enough to save you from hell. We know that faith in Jesus alone, and no works, or nothing we can do, lest we boast, can save us. Even full body dismemberment does not go far enough to atone for our sins, so this can't be literal. Jesus is using metaphors to teach. Secondly, we keep reading and He goes on to say that "it is more profitable for you that one of your members perish, than your whole body to be cast into hell". He's simply stating that anything is better than going to hell.

REMEMBER, difficulties are not contradictions.

I Peter 1:20-21;
"Knowing this first of all, that no prophecy of Scripture comes from someone's own interpretation.
For no prophecy was ever produced by the will of man, but men spoke from God as they were carried along by the Holy Spirit."

We have something more certain than an audible voice because it was written down for our scrutiny. The Revelation wasn't man-made so the interpretation is not up for grabs. We can't simply decide that because it's difficult it must therefore be contradictory or it must be allegorized. It's not and we shouldn't. God's Word is infallible - contradictions can be ruled out. In these cases we must seek the Holy Spirit for guidance. Use the whole Bible. Compare it. Connect it. Believe it!

Chapter 4

From Beginning to the End

We come to the Bible knowing there is a God.

"We come to the Bible believing it is the place where God has spoken to man, perfectly and comprehensively."
David Guzick, Enduring Word.

John 1:1-3; *"In the beginning was the Word, and the Word was with God, and the Word was God. He was in the beginning with God. All things were made through him, and without him was not any thing made that was made."*

Johns writes for us to perfectly comprehend that the Word of God is God. And Timothy warns that a time is coming (and may I be so bold to submit the time is now) when people will create their own gods with their own myths.

2 Timothy 4:3-4;

"For the time is coming when people will not endure sound teaching, but have itching ears they will accumulate for themselves teachers to suit their own passions, and will turn away from listening to the truth and wander off into myths."

Truth will (has) become distorted and people have wandered so far from God's Word and God himself. This includes the half-truth teachers because half-truth is just a false narrative the devil has deceived the masses to believe is truth. Satan is the father of lies, and he will even go so far as to use scripture to deceive even the elect (see Matt 24:24).

From; Genesis 1:1; *"In the beginning God created the heavens and the earth."*

To; Revelation 22:21; *"The grace of the Lord Jesus be with you all. Amen!"*

We follow the 100% consistency, accuracy, and fulfillment of the Glory of God in scripture. From God our Creator to Jesus our Saving Grace, the absolute brilliance of the fluidity of scripture blows my mind! Starting in Genesis, and without contradictions, through to Revelation we see the Glory of God.

If you get Genesis wrong you will get the whole Bible wrong. If you get Revelation wrong, how can you know God will keep His promises? This is why teaching the full gospel is so important. The gospel, God's redemptive plan through the Son, Jesus Christ, is found in the bible, cover to cover, not just in Matthew, Mark, Luke and John. You can not cherry pick your way through the Bible. This will create inconsistencies. This is the same when you allegorize any part of scripture. Many will take a literal approach to most of the Bible but an allegorical approach for prophecy. This is inconsistent. If you allegorize any part of scripture you automatically default to allegorical interpretation. Remember, allegorical is in essence, each man for his own interpretation. This is a very slippery slope into many false teachings.

Genesis chapter 1 tells us God spoke and created the heavens and the earths and all that dwell in it, above it, and below it in 6 days and rested on the 7th day. This is a literal 7 day creation period.

In Genesis chapter 6 we read about the flood in the days of Noah. This literally was a flood that covered the entire earth and God saved only 8 people, Noah, his wife, 3 sons and their wives.

In chapter 11 God divides the people with different languages at the tower of Babel.

Chapter 15 God establishes a covenant with Abraham, and he continues that covenant with Isaac and Jacob (later named Israel in Gen. 32:28). God will keep His promise with Israel. The church does not replace Israel. We see God's faithfulness through his promise to Israel and what a blessing it is to us that just because we disobey, God does not break His promises with us. Again, it is always all about His Glory and for His Glory.

Isaiah 48:9-11

> *"For my name's sake I defer my anger,*
> *for the sake of my praise I restrain it for you,*
> *that I may not cut you off.*
> *Behold, I have refined you in the furnace of*
> *affliction. For my own sake, for my own sake, I*
> *do it, for how should my name be profaned?*
> ***My glory I will not give to another."***

In Revelation we read about the prophecy of Christ's second coming. Here is a very quick and basic overview of the chronological events of the things to come, if we take it literally.

(NOTE: This is not an extensive outline at all. Please see book recommendations at the end of this book for further study help on end times prophecy.)

- The Rapture of the Church before the Tribulation (I Thess. 4:13-18, 5:9, Rev. 4:1)
- The (Literal) 7 year tribulation (Daniel 9:24-27) also called the time of Jacob's trouble (Jeremiah 30:7).

During the tribulation there are twenty one consecutive judgements of the wrath of God upon the earth. These are:

- 7 seal judgements (Rev 6), with the 7th seal judgment opening the 1st trumpet judgment.
- 7 trumpet judgements (Rev 8), with the 7th trumpet judgment opening the 1st bowl judgment.
- 7 bowl judgements (Rev 16) in quick succession during the second half of the tribulation.

- The rise of the antichrist, mark of the beast and abomination of desolation at the 3.5 year point (Rev 6:2, Rev 13, Dan 9:27, 12:1, Matt 24:15, Mark 13:14, II Thess 2:3-4)
- Christ's second coming with His bride, the Church, destroying the armies of the earth in the battle of Armageddon at the end of the 7 year tribulation. (Rev 19)
- Christ reigns from Jerusalem for a literal 1,000 years (millennial reign - Rev 20)
- The bounding of Satan for the millennium (Rev 20:1).
- The release of Satan for a short time at the end of the 1,000 years to deceive the nations of the world for one last fight against Christ, only to be destroyed instantly. (Rev 20:7-10)
- Satan is thrown into the lake of fire for eternity. (Rev 20:10)
- The great white throne judgment (Rev 20:11-15)
- God creates a New Heavens and New Earth for all the saints to live with Him forever and ever, amen! (Rev 21)

These are the major events in the end times as outlined by the Old Testament scholars, Jesus Himself and John in the writings of the book of Revelation.

All the Old Testament prophecies of Christ's first coming were fulfilled literally, exactly as He, through the prophets, said they would. So why then wouldn't all the prophecies of His second coming be fulfilled literally exactly as He says they will be? The events listed above from the Book of Revelation will be fulfilled literally in the "Day of the Lord".

II Thessalonians 5:2; *"For you yourselves are fully aware that the day of the Lord will come like a thief in the night."*

It is also worth noting that the Jews, concerning Jesus, missed His first coming because according to their understanding of Old Testament prophecy they were expecting the Messiah to come as a great warrior. He would stand on the Mount of Olives, defeat their enemies, and establish His Kingdom when at that time He would reign from Jerusalem and there would be peace and prosperity for Israel from that time on. Instead, He came as a baby and offered Himself up for sacrifice. With the benefit of hindsight we can look at

the Old Testament prophecies and see that His first
coming was absolutely fulfilled literally. Please
understand, that if you read eschatology (the study of
end times) literally it's clear that when Jesus comes
again He WILL come as a warrior, He WILL stand on
the Mount of Olives, He WILL destroy Israel's enemies
and He WILL establish His Kingdom here on earth for
one thousand years and reign from Jerusalem. So, they
weren't wrong, they just didn't understand that He
would come the first time for the Gentile (and the
many Jew's who would believe) and establish His
church first and will come again, for the Jew exactly as
they are expecting their Messiah and this next time they
WILL not miss it. At the second advent every Jew left
alive at the end of the seven year tribulation will bow to
Jesus and confess Him the Son of David, The Christ,
The Messiah. At that point God will have fulfilled His
promises to Abraham, Isaaac and Jacob, His covenant
with Israel. It's perfect and it's a divine plan that God
has been working on since the very beginning.

Throughout the Bible we see the brilliance of the
intricacies of Christ's redemptive plan for Israel and for
both Jew and Gentile. In the four gospels located in
the New Testament we witness the birth of our Lord
and Savior Jesus Christ, that was prophesied in the Old

Testament along with his death on the cross, the only perfect Lamb of God worthy to take away the sins of the world. Now through His resurrection He has made a way, bridged the gap, paid the full price of our sin so that we might have eternal life in Christ. Glory to God our Savior Jesus Christ!

Romans 5:9;
"Since, therefore, we have now been justified by his blood, much more shall we be saved by him from the wrath of God."

This is the blessed hope we have in Him. He paid the price so that all who repent, and accept His forgiveness through faith in Christ Jesus will be saved from the wrath of God and spend eternity with Him.

Romans 3:23-26;
"For all have sinned and fall short of the glory of God, and are justified by his grace as a gift, through the redemption that is in Christ Jesus, whom God put forward as a propitiation by his blood, to be received by faith. This was to show God's righteousness, because in his divine forbearance he had passed over former sins. It was to show his righteousness at the present time, so that

he might be just and the justifier of the one who has faith in Jesus.

From beginning to the end, we have this testimony in Christ, that He is faithful in His promises. We look for Jesus in Genesis, just as we look for Jesus in Revelation. It's all about Jesus.

And since I am on a Romans kick for this chapter, I will end this one with Romans 5:1-2; *"Therefore, since we have been justified by faith, we have peace with God through our Lord Jesus Christ. Through him we have also obtained access by faith into this grace in which we stand, and we rejoice in hope of the glory of God."*

Chapter 5

The Lens With Which We View And Understand Everything

2 Corinthians 10:3;
"For though we walk in the flesh, we are not waging war according to the flesh."

If you haven't already figured out what the "lens" with which we view and understand everything is, the lens is the Bible. This is the whole premise of this book. To press the importance of reading and understanding the Word of God. Scripture is our ultimate guide in this crazy world we are living in. It is the foundation of truth because it is THE TRUTH. We need to filter every single word against the Word of God. Stop depending on a pastor, or a podcastor, or an influencer, or an author to filter what is happening in and around this world. Fact check everyone and everything with scripture. If you are not reading scripture daily, and seeking to obey scripture, and meditating on it day and night, you will be a neon flashing target for the devil to deceive you.

Ephesians 6:10-12;
"Finally, be strong in the Lord and in the strength of his might. Put on the whole armor of God, that you may be able to stand against the schemes of the devil. For we do not wrestle against flesh and blood, but against the rulers, against the authorities, against the cosmic powers over this present darkness, against the spiritual forces of evil in the heavenly places."

Do you understand the severity of the words in this scripture? This is not a battle of the flesh. It is not about your physical suffering, or some first world inconveniences but this is about an all out blood thirsty spiritual war with a very dark and evil devil who is after your soul. The only protection you have is found in the WORD OF GOD! Don't be too "busy", too lazy, or too indifferent to pick up your Bible daily and armor up! Your life depends on it!

Ephesians 6:13-20 continues;
"Therefore take up the whole armor of God, that you may be able to withstand in the evil day, and having

done all, to stand firm. Stand therefore, having fastened on the belt of truth, and having put on the breastplate of righteousness, and, as shoes for your feet, having put on the readiness given by the gospel of peace. In all circumstances take up the shield of faith, with which you can extinguish all the flaming darts of the evil one; and take the helmet of salvation, and the sword of the Spirit, which is the word of God, praying at all times in the Spirit, with prayer and supplication. To that end keep alert with all perseverance, making supplication for all the saints, and also for me (Paul), that words may be given to me in opening my mouth boldly to proclaim the mystery of the gospel, for which I am an ambassador in chains, that I may declare it boldly, as I ought to speak."

I feel as though this scripture could take a lifetime to fully comprehend and at the same time it is literally so simple and gives us clear instructions and warning. Using this scripture as your "lens", look at the twisted world around you that has blurred the truth to the point of indecipherable, and see where your armor is missing and where you need to secure up your spiritual armor. We call ourselves Christians, but do you know what Christian means? Soldiers for Christ (2 Timothy 2:3 *you therefore must endure hardship as a good soldier of Jesus Christ*). <u>Are you headed to battle fully armored</u>

<u>*for* Christ, *with* Christ, and *in* Christ? Every piece of armor is Christ!</u>

Make sure your lenses are washed and cleaned with the blood of Jesus Christ, and you are seeing The Truth clearly.

Ask yourself, could I discern truth from almost truth?

This is Satan's favorite line, "Did God really say?"
Genesis 3:1-2; *Now the serpent was more crafty than any other beast of the field that the Lord God had made.*
He said to the woman, "Did God actually say, 'You shall not eat of any tree in the garden?"

And then, after he plants the seed of doubt and confusion, he twists the truth just slightly enough for it to be a complete lie but without knowing God's Word you just might believe it as "truth".

Genesis 3:4-5; *But the serpent said to the woman, "You will not surely die. For God knows that when you eat of it your eyes will be opened, and you will be like God, knowing good and evil."*

These lies can sound like truths especially when they come out of the mouths of pastors and other "respected" teachers of faith. Test everything against scripture. EVERYTHING.

1 John 4:1; *Beloved, do not believe every spirit, but test the spirits to see whether they are from God, for many false prophets have gone out into the world.*

1 John 4:2; *By this you know the Spirit of God: every spirit that confesses that Jesus Christ has come in the flesh is from God.*

The Holy Spirit and God's infallible Word will help you discern the spirits.

1 John 4:4-6; *Little children, you are from God and have overcome them, for he who is in you is greater than he who is in the world. They are from the world; therefore they speak from the world, and the world listens to them. We are from God. Whoever knows God listens to us; whoever is not from God does not listen to us. By this we know the Spirit of Truth and the spirit of error.*

Chapter 6

Jesus Wins!

The good news is that Jesus wins! He has conquered sin and death!

There is no greater journey than the pursuit of God. The future is upon us and we are headed into it and it will overtake everyone. It is literal and inevitable. **But God** wants to be our guide, our leader, our companion, our compass, and our protector. He has equipped (us) His children with every Spiritual blessing we need in Him for this journey. He has gone before us, He is the First and the Last, the Alpha and the Omega, the Beginning and the End. Stay encouraged and filled with hope. And;

READ YOUR BIBLE!

Revelation 1:8; *"I am the Alpha and the Omega," says the Lord God, "who is and who was and who is to come, the Almighty."*

Revelation 21:6; *And he said to me, "It is done! I am the Alpha and the Omega, the beginning and the end. To the thirsty I will give from the spring of the water of life without payment."*

Revelation 22:1; *"I am the Alpha and the Omega, the first and the last, the beginning and the end."*

Jesus is coming soon. Are you ready to stand before Him?

He who testifies to these things says, "Surely I am coming soon." Amen. Come, Lord Jesus. Revelation 22:20

Maranatha!

Chapter 7

Reading Through The Bible Plans

Don't wait, start reading your Bible today!

There are many different Bible reading plans, such as, reading chronologically through the Bible as historically written, or reading cover to cover as your Bible is layed out. There are many different printable tools you can find on the internet to help you stay on track and track your progress. I highly suggest using one.

The QR code at the end of this book will take you to my website that will have a saveable and printable pdf copy. The main thing is DON'T WAIT, START TODAY!

Most reading plans are designed to read through the Bible in a year. It is no small feat but it is extremely doable. Remember, to look for Jesus and see His Glory on every page.

Epilogue

Thank you for taking the time to read this book.
If you have never received Christ as your Lord and
Savior and repented of your sins, I encourage you
to do so today.

Pray this prayer with me:

Dear Jesus, I acknowledge that I am a sinner in
need of a Savior. I confess my sins and ask for
your forgiveness. I believe you died on the cross
for my sins, Jesus, and God raised you from the
dead. Please come into my heart. I want to live
for you. Thank you Jesus. In your name, Jesus,
Amen.

Romans 10:9-10
*Because, if you confess with your mouth that Jesus is Lord
and believe in your heart that God raised him from the
dead, you will be saved.*
*For with the heart one believes and is justified, and with
the mouth one confesses and is saved.*

Book Recommendations

Please check out my website,
www.theliteralword.com for recommended books,
bible reading plans and other resources.

Scan the QR code below with your smartphone camera
for a link to the website.

References

Advance Notice: Jesus Wins! By Mark Fischer, 2012

Enduring Word Bible Commentary, By David Guzik

The Bible, ESV English Standard Version 2007 by Crossway Bibles, Good New publishers ministry.

Made in the USA
Columbia, SC
19 May 2024

35474268R00026